Wild WATER

Canoeing and Kayaking

ADVENTURE OUTDOORS

NEIL CHAMPION

W
FRANKLIN WATTS
LONDON•SYDNEY

 An Appleseed Editions book

First published in 2012 by Franklin Watts
338 Euston Road, London NW1 3BH

Franklin Watts Australia
Hachette Children's Books
Level 17/207 Kent St, Sydney, NSW 2000

© 2012 Appleseed Editions

Created by Appleseed Editions Ltd,
Well House, Friars Hill, Guestling,
East Sussex TN35 4ET

Designed and illustrated by Guy Callaby
Edited by Mary-Jane Wilkins
Picture research by Su Alexander

ISBN 978 1 4451 0969 5

Dewey Classification: 797.1 '22

A CIP catalogue for this book is available
from the British Library.

Picture credits
l = left, r = right, c = centre, t = top, b = bottom

Page 1 Jupiterimages/Thinkstock; 2,4,5,6 & 7t Thinkstock; 7b Wikimedia
Commons/Ruth Crafer; 8t Oleg Zabielin/Shutterstock, c Brian Lasenby/
Shutterstock, b Thinkstock; 9 Chudakov/Shutterstock; 10 Jupiterimages/
Thinkstock; 13t Thinkstock, b Wikimedia Commons/P J Blalock;
14 Thomas Northcut/Thinkstock; 15t Thinkstock, b Chudakov/
Shutterstock; 17 Lane V Erickson/Shutterstock; 18 David Kay/
Shutterstock; 19l Mark Yuill/Shutterstock, r Comstock/Thinkstock;
20 Falk Kienas/Shutterstock; 21 Thinkstock; 22 Hemera Technologies/
Thinkstock; 23 Mike Powell/Thinkstock; 24 Comstock Images/
Thinkstock; 25l Klaitu/Shutterstock, r Thomas Northcut/Thinkstock;
26 Vince Clements/Shutterstock; 27l Hemera Technologies/
Thinkstock, r Thinkstock; 28 Thinkstock; 29t Wikimedia Commons/
National Geographic volume 31 1917/George R King,
b Vereshchagin Dmitry/Shutterstock; 31 Marekuliasz/Shutterstock;
32t Thinkstock, b Jupiterimages/Thinkstock:

Front cover: Monkey Business Images/Shutterstock

Printed in Singapore

Franklin Watts is a division
of Hachette Children's Books,
an Hachette UK company.
www.hachette.co.uk

Contents

Let's go paddling!

Earth is a very wet place. Its rivers, lakes and seas provide us with food and ways of moving around, as well as adventure and fun.

The Inuit (the native peoples of the Arctic) were the first to move around on water in small boats called kayaks. Their small, one-person boats navigated the waterways of Canada and Greenland, where ice often blocks the way. The Inuit covered their boats with a tight skin to keep water out – today this is called a **spraydeck**. Other native peoples around the world used open canoes in less extreme conditions. The skills they developed have made canoeing and kayaking popular water sports. Wherever you live, you can enjoy learning to paddle.

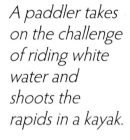

A paddler takes on the challenge of riding white water and shoots the rapids in a kayak.

Learning to kayak in the controlled environment of an indoor pool.

Rising to the challenge

Imagine you're in a small boat on a river, nearing some rapids. White water swirls around you, drawing your boat towards rocks and whirlpools. You have to paddle skilfully to avoid them. Then you're shooting along mid-stream with running water all around. Can you stay in control? What's coming up?

This is when you draw on the skills you've learned in training: steering, using the paddle to bypass danger and staying upright. You remember what to do if you **capsize**. Your heart is pounding and **adrenalin** pumps round your body. You are ready for the challenge!

Levels of risk

Adventure sports test your skill and knowledge against the risks of taking part. You have to make sure you are skilled enough to take on the challenge. Too little challenge might be boring. Too much could frighten you and put you at risk. The right level allows you to be a happy, adrenalin-fuelled adventurer.

DID YOU KNOW?

The oldest canoe ever found is around 10,000 years old. It was **excavated** in the Netherlands. The word canoe means 'dugout'; the first canoes were dug out of a tree trunk. The Inuit have used kayaks for 4,000 years. Kayak means 'hunter's boat' and Inuit hunters used them to catch large sea creatures – even whales.

Getting started

Learning how to stay upright in a boat and paddle it along takes practice and patience. Start by asking for advice from experienced friends, or at a canoe or kayaking club at school or where you live.

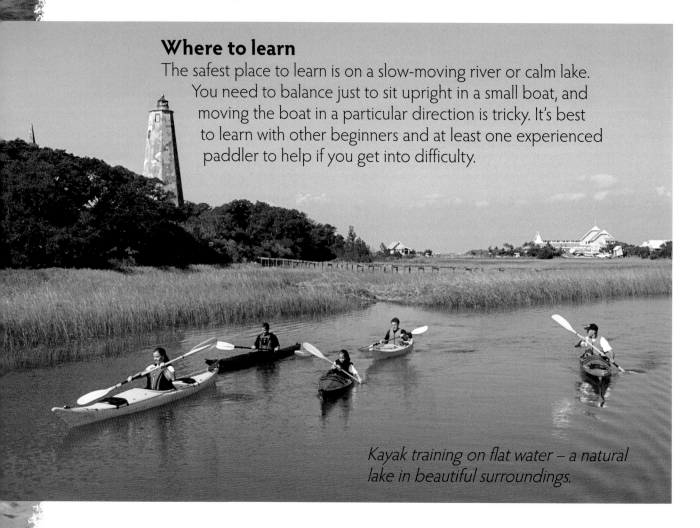

Where to learn

The safest place to learn is on a slow-moving river or calm lake. You need to balance just to sit upright in a small boat, and moving the boat in a particular direction is tricky. It's best to learn with other beginners and at least one experienced paddler to help if you get into difficulty.

Kayak training on flat water – a natural lake in beautiful surroundings.

Capsizing

Before you start, make sure you can swim at least 50 metres in your clothes – that's harder than it sounds! Then start by learning what to do if you capsize, so you can relax a bit, knowing you'll be able to cope with whatever happens.

What to wear

On a warm day with warm water and fine weather, wear shorts and a T-shirt with a **flotation vest** or buoyancy aid. On colder days you'll need a **thermal layer** next to the skin and a **cagoule** with sealed cuffs and neck openings to stop water getting in. Paddlers often wear a wetsuit. Trainers are fine on your feet, although tech sandals or water-sport shoes are better. A helmet is essential for white water to protect your face and head if you hit the boat or rocks.

Flotation vests and helmets are essential safety gear for kayakers.

Amazing FACTS

The longest solo kayaking journey ever made on a river was along the mighty River Amazon in Brazil, South America. The British children's TV presenter, Helen Skelton, paddled more than 3,000 km in 2010. She also set the record for the longest distance covered in 24 hours by a woman –121 km – and paddled an amazing average of 96.5 km a day.

7

Boats and Water

Boats range from a two-person slim sea kayak to the small, rounder stunt craft used in wild white water. If you plan to buy a boat, find out about the different types and talk to as many experienced people as you can first.

This is a kayak...

Canoe or kayak?

A canoe and a kayak look very similar. Both are small boats, in which paddlers face the way they are going (unlike rowers, who face backwards). You sit inside a kayak and paddle with a double-bladed paddle. In a canoe you either sit or kneel and paddle with a single-bladed paddle or pole.

...and this is a canoe.

DID YOU KNOW?

Native peoples made the first kayaks and canoes from wood bark, bone and animal skins – even whole tree trunks sometimes.

A traditional Polynesian canoe.

White water

One of the toughest places to paddle a small boat is a fast-running river. Rivers with a **gradient** big enough to allow the water to form rapids are called white water. The churning water gives kayakers and canoeists a thrilling ride. White water rivers are graded depending on how tough they are, ranging from grade 1 to grade 6.

Grade 6 rivers have large rapids and big drops between hazards.

Before you have a go at even a grade 1 river, you need good paddling skills, as well as a good understanding of your boat.

White-water grades for rivers

Grade 1 Easy. Slow-moving water with small waves; no serious obstacles.

Grade 2 Medium. Moderate rapids and other hazards.

Grade 3 Difficult. High waves, larger rapids and other hazards. Check out the route first.

Grade 4 Very difficult. Long rapids and high waves. Dangerous hazards including rocks, strong **eddies** and **undercurrents**. You need to be an expert with an excellent boat and quality equipment.

Grade 5 Extremely difficult. Long, violent rapids, one after the other; big drops and strong currents; very steep gradient; extreme hazards with narrow sections.

Grade 6 Very few people tackle this level. The water is so violent, and the drops so large, that there is a real danger of dying.

Boat design

Large, stable two-person sea kayaks can travel long distances and carry heavy loads: tents, food, cookers and more. They are easy to handle, comfortable and cope with sea **swells**. At the other extreme are stunt boats: small and unstable, but easy to handle.

This family is loading a large canoe and supplies ready for a holiday on the river.

Modern kayaks

A basic modern kayak is about four metres long and 60 cm at its widest. It is light and low in the water, with a pointed end to help carve a path. Today most boats of this sort are made of plastic.

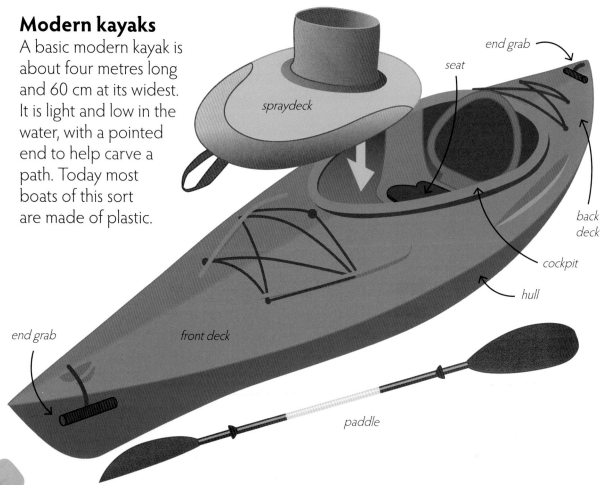

spraydeck

end grab

seat

back deck

cockpit

hull

end grab

front deck

paddle

Open canoes

These boats have changed little from their original design, when they were used by native Americans and Canadians to travel around waterways and carry goods. Today holidaymakers still go on camping and touring trips in canoes.

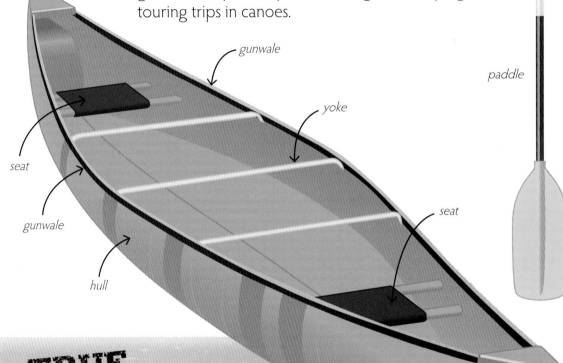

stern

gunwale

yoke

seat

gunwale

hull

seat

bow

keel

paddle

TRUE Survivors

In 1793, Scottish fur trader Alexander Mackenzie crossed the Rocky Mountains (in north west Canada) to reach the Pacific Ocean, in a canoe with a small team of men. He was the first to do this. He set out from Lake Athabasca in the centre of Canada and covered 3,000 km of wilderness, paddling upstream as well as down and carrying his canoe between rivers. Two hundred years later

British poet and adventurer Robert Twigger made the same trip. He faced the same hazards – isolation, food shortage, attack by bears, getting lost, tackling white water rapids and avoiding injury. His traditional birch bark canoes stitched together with pine roots, is on display in the Peace River Town Museum, in Alberta, Canada.

Danger in the water!

Paddlers need to know the hazards they are likely to meet, whether they're paddling in a river, lake or the sea.

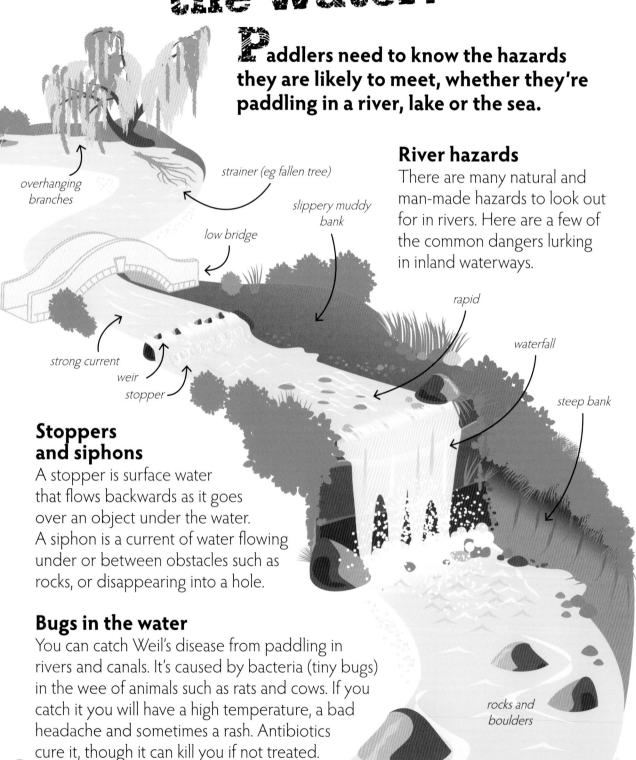

overhanging branches

strainer (eg fallen tree)

slippery muddy bank

low bridge

strong current

weir

stopper

rapid

waterfall

steep bank

rocks and boulders

River hazards

There are many natural and man-made hazards to look out for in rivers. Here are a few of the common dangers lurking in inland waterways.

Stoppers and siphons

A stopper is surface water that flows backwards as it goes over an object under the water. A siphon is a current of water flowing under or between obstacles such as rocks, or disappearing into a hole.

Bugs in the water

You can catch Weil's disease from paddling in rivers and canals. It's caused by bacteria (tiny bugs) in the wee of animals such as rats and cows. If you catch it you will have a high temperature, a bad headache and sometimes a rash. Antibiotics cure it, though it can kill you if not treated.

Storms at sea are a hazard to paddlers.

Lakes and seas

When you're paddling on a large lake or in the sea, you can lose sight of land. At sea, an offshore wind can make it hard to paddle back to shore, as can an outgoing tide. Always carry a map, a whistle and **flares** to attract attention.

Watch the weather

Always get a weather forecast, especially if you are going any distance from shore. Strong wind, rain, hot sun or a big drop in temperature can all lead to problems.

TRUE Survivors

Tyler Bradt is a 26-year-old American white water kayaker. In April 2009 he broke the world record for the longest waterfall drop – a staggering 57 metres over the Palouse Falls in Washington State, USA. It took him four seconds in free-fall to hit the water at the bottom. Bradt had trained for this feat by kayaking over bigger and bigger falls. He knew that Palouse would be more complicated than any previous waterfall. Bradt was supported by a team of nine people, including two in boats at the bottom of the fall in case he needed to be rescued. He never doubted that he could do it, even during the heart-stopping seconds when he was paddling towards the lip of the fall. "Palouse was a calculated risk, no doubt dangerous, but also one of the most amazing days of my life."

13

Learning to kayak

Start from a place where it is easy to get into your boat, such as a flat water river or a lake with a bank or **jetty**. Once you are launched, stay in sight of the place you can get out again. Do not go alone; make sure there are two other boats with you, to help if you get into trouble.

Getting into a kayak

Draw your boat to the bank. Hold it with one hand and the bank with your other. Swing one leg into the cockpit, move forward, pull in your other leg and sit down. Hold the bank to steady the boat, reach for your paddle and put it across the boat ready to use. Fix your spraydeck in place.

A paddler launches his boat from a river bank where there is flat water.

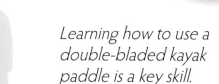

First steps

A kayak paddle has a **blade** at both ends. It should be the right length: if it's too long it will be hard to handle, and if it's too short you won't get enough power from it. When you rest one end of the paddle on the ground, the other end should be about 30 cm above your head. Make sure you sit upright with your feet against the footrest, legs bent and knees against the side of the boat.

30 cm

Learning how to use a double-bladed kayak paddle is a key skill.

Paddle strokes

Forward paddle

Reach forward, keep the paddle close to the boat and sticking up in the air (see left). Use your body to move you forwards.

Backward paddle

Turn your shoulders, reach back with the paddle and keep your arms as straight as possible. Try to keep in a straight line.

Stopping the boat

When moving forward, put the blade into the water at about 90° to your boat. You should feel the pressure of the water against it. Then put the other blade into the water to slow down more and stop you turning.

AMAZING KAYAK MARATHON

Ian Tordoff kayaked across the English Channel from Folkestone, Kent, to Wisant Beach near Calais in northern France in 3 hours 22 minutes in May 2005. He beat a world record that had stood for nearly 30 years. Then, in October 2007, Olympic champion Ian Wynne broke Tordoff's record by making the crossing in 2 hours 59 minutes and 6 seconds.

Learning to canoe

Open canoes are great for family camping trips as you can store lots of kit in them. Make sure your canoe is watertight so no spray comes in. Experienced paddlers can tackle quite rough water in an open canoe, but when you are learning, make sure you stay on flat water.

Getting into a canoe

When you try to step into an open canoe the boat will move away from the shore. Pull it to the shore and hold the near side with your paddle placed across it. Then take hold of the other side of the boat and step lightly in. Now sit or kneel.

Sit or kneel?

Kneeling gives you better control over the boat and allows you to make stronger strokes. Keep your back straight and your knees braced against the side of the boat. Sit so your weight makes the front of the boat (the bow) rise a little out of the water. This helps you move the boat around more easily.

Paddling

A canoe paddle should come up to your chin. An open canoe paddle has one blade and is shorter than a kayak paddle. Make the strokes by putting one hand on top and the other on the **shaft**, level with the edge of the boat. Keep the paddle as close to the boat as possible. Two people can paddle together; put the lightest person in front so the boat lifts a little.

Paddle on both sides when trying to travel in a straight line in a large open canoe.

AMAZING CANOE MARATHON

The longest non-stop, two-person canoe race in America is held every year in July. The Au Sable River International Canoe Marathon covers 193 km, starting in Grayling and finishing in Oscoda on Lake Huron, in Michigan, USA. The race starts at 9.00 pm. Around 100 competitors run through the streets of Grayling carrying their boats. Then they paddle through the night (between 14 and 19 hours) to reach the finish.

During the race competitors paddle at about 60 strokes a minute – making around 60,000 strokes in total. The race is one of the toughest endurance events in the world and the winner earns prize money of more than $50,000 (about £30,000). The fastest time for completing the race was 14 hours 8 minutes 18 seconds, set by Canadian Serge Corbin and his American partner, Jeff Kolka, in 1999.

White Water

The biggest challenge in paddling is white water. This can mean shooting the rapids on a river or taking on waves and surf at sea. Whichever form it takes, white water paddling spells excitement and danger.

Grade 5 white water presents a serious challenge for paddlers.

Never take on something you don't think you can handle. You need to know the grading system for rivers (see page 9), and learn how to look at a river and 'read it'. This means finding a safe route through waves, stoppers, drops and **strainers**. Remember that rivers can rise or fall: heavy rain, melting snow and hydro-electric power stations can all change a gently flowing river into a raging torrent. Storms out at sea can send a large swell towards land which whips up larger waves than usual.

Equipment

Apart from your boat and paddle (both should be quite short), you will need a helmet to protect your head from rocks, a flotation vest, a **throw-line** and a knife.

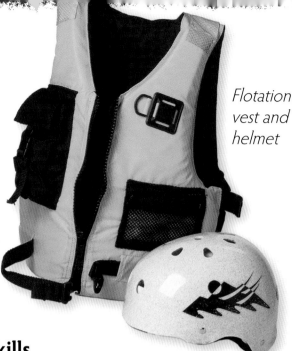

Flotation vest and helmet

White-water skills

Before taking on your first white-water river, you must have mastered all the basic paddle strokes. You need to be able to do an emergency roll and right the boat, or remove the spraydeck and make a wet water exit and swim. You should also know how to help rescue a paddler in trouble. Never paddle white water alone and make sure the distance to the next safe place to get out of the water is not too great.

Amazing FACTS

The Niagara Gorge below the Niagara Falls in North America holds one of the hardest grade 6 rapids in the world. More than 3,000 tonnes of water sweep over the falls every minute into the raging river below. This stretch of water has a whirlpool 150m deep, and a section of water called the Himalayas because the standing waves are so big (up to 6m high). Americans Chris Spelius and Ken Lagergren were the first to kayak down the gorge in the 1970s. The first woman to shoot these rapids was the American Carrie Ashton, in the early 1980s.

Emergency on the river!

Even with the best preparation, things can go wrong. Paddlers can be injured, difficult conditions can tire you, or you might capsize and need help to get back into your boat or to the shore. You need to know what to do if any of these things happen to you or someone in your group.

Capsize drill

🌢 You must wear a flotation vest to keep you afloat.

🌢 When upside down under water, lean forward with the paddle alongside the boat.

🌢 Move the front paddle blade across the body and on to the surface of the water.

🌢 At the same time, twist the upper body and hips and use the paddle to push the boat upright with you still in it.

🌢 When you come to the surface, you should be leaning backwards in the boat.

Knowing how to roll upright after capsizing is a key skill which paddlers should learn early on.

Wet exits

Learn how to roll or get out of a boat in calm water first, before you try it on wild water. If you cannot roll, you will have to make a wet exit and swim out.

To do this in an open canoe, stay in the boat until you are completely underwater. This prevents you being hit by the boat as it turns over. Kick with your feet and push with your hands to get away, but try to hold on to the paddle. As you come up, take hold of the boat too. Alternatively, jump out of the boat before it turns over. Practise both methods.

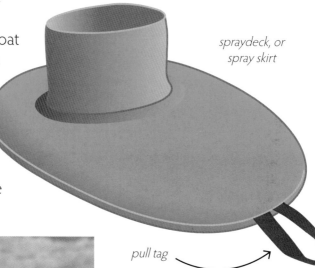

spraydeck, or spray skirt

pull tag

If your kayak has a spraydeck, grab the pull tag that releases it, so you won't be trapped under the boat. Practise finding the tag with your eyes closed. Once you are free of the spraydeck, push out of the boat and swim to the surface.

Towing

Learn how to tow a boat and paddler to safety. There are several ways of doing this.

Extreme conditions require excellent skills. Make sure you are up to the challenges you take on.

Sea kayaking

Imagine floating on a calm sea, with the shore never far away, exploring hidden beaches and caves that few people have seen. This is the lure of sea kayaking – freedom, exploration, exercise and fun! Before you go out, check the weather, tides and the sea. Be prepared for the worst and you will have a good time.

Safety first

Never go kayaking alone. Sea kayaks can seat one or two people, but make sure you go with at least two other boats. You never know what might happen. If the paddlers in one boat tire, the others may need to tow them to shore.

What to take with you

Sea kayaks are longer than white water boats (4 metres rather than 2.5 metres). They need to be stable and to have storage space for extra kit – clothes, food, water, a tent and a cooker. You also need a good map and compass and to know how to read them.

There is safety in numbers. This group is heading off together for the coast.

Global positioning systems (**GPS**) can be very accurate and a useful backup. Other equipment should include a flotation vest, a safety flare in case of emergency, and a first aid kit.

TRUE Survivors

Aleksander Doba from Poland made the longest solo kayaking voyage ever in 2010. On 26 October Doba set off in his kayak from Dakar, in Senegal, to paddle across the Atlantic Ocean to Brazil. During the trip he encountered some tricky weather conditions, including such extreme heat that he could only paddle by night, and winds which sent him round in circles. Doba eventually arrived in the mouth of the river Acarau in Brazil 99 days later and 14 kilos lighter, having covered 5,394 km. What makes Doba's feat of strength and endurance all the greater is the fact that he was 64 years old at the time. His other achievements include being the first person to circumnavigate the Baltic Sea and Baikal Lake, as well as the first to paddle the entire length of the Polish coast in both directions.

Going on a journey

Planning and going on a journey can be great fun, whether you spend just one night in a tent on the beach or take a week-long trip far from civilization.

TRUE Survivors

An inexperienced couple set off in a canoe along a ten kilometre stretch of the Snake River in Minnesota, USA. They thought it would take about three hours to reach a place where they could get out of the river again, so they set off around midday. They took few clothes (it was warm) and only matches for emergency gear. But the river was low and sluggish and the journey took much longer than expected. They had only travelled six kilometres when the sun began to set and the temperature started to fall, making them dangerously cold.

At this point they spotted a dim light on the river bank. They struggled out of the water and found help in a small cabin. The couple were lucky that someone was there to help them. If you listed all the things they did wrong on this trip, the list would be quite a long one!

Guides and equipment

River guide books will tell you about the **code of conduct** for the river, as well as important features, white water grades, places where you can launch your boat and places where you will need to carry the boat (called portage).

These paddlers are carrying their boat to avoid a hazard such as big rapids or waterfalls.

Before setting out on a trip, make sure that everyone is suitably equipped and let someone know your planned route in case of emergency.

Entering competitions

There are many types of competition you can take part in with a kayak or canoe.

Paddlers compete in river races on flat or white water, slaloms, **freestyle races**, sprints and marathons. You can play canoe polo or enter kayak surfing competitions.

The Olympics

Kayaks and canoes became part of the Olympic Games in 1936. Since then, the best paddlers in the world have competed at the summer games, held every four years. Olympic events include the 500 metre and 1,000 metre sprint. There can be solo paddlers, two or even four people in a boat. Heats are held, with the winners going forward each time.

This man is taking part in an Olympic white water slalom competition.

TRUE SPORTSMAN

Sweden's top paddler is Anders Gustafsson, born in Jönköping in 1979. He started canoeing at seven and was spotted by the Swedish Olympic Committee in 1999. At the time he was in the Swedish army, working as a personal guard of the king. Gustafsson took part in his first Olympic games in Sydney in 2000 and has since become a full-time champion sprint canoeist. What makes him so good? Being 1.92m tall helps; his long arms and legs help to power his strokes when kayaking. He trains hard and long to improve his skills and fitness.

Slalom racing

The slalom is an exciting event held on a 300-metre artificial white water course. Competitors paddle around a series of up to 25 gates and receive penalties if they touch them. The challenge is to master the wild water while weaving in and out of the gates, finishing in as fast a time as you can. No race is more thrilling to watch than the slalom!

One of the most extreme canoe races is the Quebec ice canoe race, held every year in Canada. Teams of five compete to be the first to cross the St Lawrence river, battling strong currents, high tides and ice floes.

AMAZING SPRINT RECORDS

Here are some world records set by solo canoeists and kayakers in international canoe and kayaking competitions.

Men's 500 metres record
1 minute, 34.68 seconds, set by Anders Gustafsson of Sweden in 2009.

Women's 500 metres record
1 minute 47.343 seconds, set by Katalin Kovacs of Hungary in 2002.

Men's 1,000 metres record
3 minutes 22.484 seconds, set by Max Hoff of Germany in 2011.

Women's 1,000 metres record
3 minutes 52.983 seconds, set by Elzbieta Urbanczik of Poland in 2001.

27

What do you know about paddling?

Do you think you're ready to venture on to the water? Do you know the difference between a sea kayak and a white water boat? What equipment do you need on a long journey and how do you escape from a capsized boat? Try this quiz to find out how much you know about paddling. Answers on page 31.

1 How many grades are there in white water paddling?
a Ten
b Twelve
c Six
d Three

2 When you capsize your boat and are underwater, what should you do?
a Hold your breath and wait for rescue.
b Remove any obstacles, push out of the boat and swim to the surface.
c Let go of your paddle to let people know you are in trouble.
d Take off your flotation vest.

1

2

3

▶ **3** Link these images to their names.
a Weir
b Stopper
c Strainer
d Waterfall
e Rapids

4

5

◀ **4** The native peoples of the Arctic invented the kayak. True or false?

5 What is a spraydeck for?
a Cleaning your boat.
b Keeping water out of the cockpit.
c Storing extra kit.
d Keeping your pack of cards dry.

6 What is a buoyancy aid (flotation vest) for?
a Keeping you afloat if your boat capsizes.
b Keeping your boat upright in wild water.
c Helping you to get into your boat.
d Mending a hole in your boat.

7 What is a siphon?
a A small bottle for keeping your drink in.
b A small tube for getting water out of your boat.
c A place where water disappears underground and presents a hazard to paddlers.
d A sign that paddlers put on their boats.

8 What is the name of the disease you can catch from paddling in some canals and rivers?
a Influenza
b Scarlet fever
c Lyme disease
d Weil's disease

9 Which of these items should you take paddling when the weather is forecast to be cold?
a Wetsuit or cagoule
b Thermal layer
c Shorts
d Sun hat

▶ **10** Link the following items to their names
a End grab
b Hull
c Cockpit
d Front deck
e Bow
f Stern

Glossary

adrenalin A chemical our bodies make to help us run fast from danger or fight it.

blade The part of a paddle that goes in the water to move the boat along.

cagoule A windproof and waterproof jacket.

capsize To turn upside down in a boat on a river or at sea.

code of conduct A set of guidelines to help people use the river responsibly and consider other users.

eddies Patches of river water that flow in a circle, often beside a main current or downstream of an obstacle such as a rock.

excavated Dug out of the ground.

flare A device used in an emergency at sea. A flare gives off a bright light and smoke to attract attention.

flotation vest A piece of equipment (also called a buoyancy aid) made from light material that keeps you afloat.

freestyle races A competition held on white water. Competitors perform acrobatic moves in small boats. It is also called playboating.

gradient The angle of a river bed. A steep gradient means waterfalls and rapids form. A gentle gradient means the river moves slowly.

GPS A Global Positioning System is a hand-held device used to find out where you are and to navigate. It works by fixing on three or more satellites as they orbit the Earth.

jetty A structure that sticks out into a river, lake or sea from which you can launch a boat.

shaft The handle of a paddle.

spraydeck A tight-fitting cover that goes over you and the cockpit of your kayak. It stops water spray getting into the boat.

strainer A hazard such as a tree with lots of branches sticking out of a river. Water is 'strained' through the hazard, but a boat would get trapped.

swell The rising and falling of the sea is called the swell. After a storm there can be a very big swell.

thermal layer A layer of clothing worn next to the skin to keep you warm and dry. Clothes made of wool and some artificial fibres make good thermal layers.

throw-line A line usually between 10 and 25 metres long, used in an emergency to throw to someone in difficulty in the water.

undercurrents Water under the surface that moves in a particular direction. Undercurrents can be dangerous because you cannot always see them.

weir A small dam or barrier in a river which slows the flow of water. Weirs can be hazardous to paddlers.

Websites

American Canoe Association www.americancanoe.org
Australian Canoeing www.canoe.org.au
British Canoe Union www.bcu.org.uk
Irish Canoe Union www.irishcanoeunion.com
New Zealand Canoe Federation www.canoenz.org.nz
The Scottish Canoe Association www.canoescotland.org
Welsh Canoeing www.canoewales.com

Books

Basic Canoeing John Round, Stackpole Books, 2003
Kayaking and Canoeing Paul Mason, A&C Black, 2011
Kayaking and Canoeing for Beginners Bill Mattos, Southwater, 2004

Quiz answers

1 *c*

2 *b*

3 *1:d, 2:c, 3:a, 4:e, 5:b*

4 *True*

5 *b*

6 *a*

7 *c*

8 *d*

9 *a & b*

10 *1:c, 2:e, 3:d, 4:a, 5:f, 6:b.*

Index